The Second Wind
The Immortal Wind

Eric Blau

Collected Poems
1943 -1998

B&B First Editions

 Published by
B&B First Editions

For Alexander, my father, and
Julia, my mother

For my sons, John, Peter, and Matthew.
And for Paul who is no longer with us

For my sister, Lillian

For my granddaughters Juliana, Clarissa
and their mother, Cora

For Iris, Paul's daughter

For Elly Stone, my wife.

Edited by Lily Turner

Cover design: Roy Doty
Cover Photo: Stewart Geldin
Art Director: Robert Louis Banov

Today I wrote my own obit.
Some of it true, most of it shit.

E.B.

CONTENTS

ACKNOWLEDGMENTS

Many thanks to —

My old friend the great poet Tom McGrath, departed, from whose work I sometimes quote.

Angela Darling, who dealt with the manuscript and made me rethink where periods and semicolons go.

Robert Louis Banov, the Publisher who believes in poetry.

And especially to my friend Hank Hoffman, whose endless flow of ironies serves to keep me honest, and who said, after I read him one of the pieces which make up this collection: "Yeah, but does it read as well as it sounds?"

E.B.

INTRODUCTION

I don't know when I started writing poetry. (I am including here verse generally, lyrics, doggerel, rhymed things.) I was a very young child, just outgrowing my crib. My sister Lillian, two years my senior, says she remembers me at that early time reciting my first work. *Sunny days/You got golden flies/About your face.* I have repeated those lines throughout my life. Not because they are good but rather that the lines are like a lock of hair or a soft shoe saved from a time scarcely remembered. Or perhaps remembered so deeply that the golden flies still cling to a summer window pane in an old tenement building on Ninth Street, part of New York's hallowed Lower East Side.

I have wondered what brought poetry things out of my mouth. My father did not introduce me to that kind of language, although he sang around the house: Hungarian songs, pop folk of a kind. *(Lari, Lari, nem kel varni/Frish esh jol a chol/ Chokalosni/chokalosni, jol, jol, jol/* Lari, Lari, you don't have to wait/your kisses are fresh and good/

So kiss, kiss, good, good, good.) I think my father Alexander, in those early days was still flirting with Julia, my pretty mother.

We had no radio (1924, 1925). Did my sister also sing? Did my mother? But it must have been in that period that the idea of language making a music got implanted in me. So even now, having reached my seventy-seventh birthday I find myself improvising little poems as I walk along Broadway. Poems which I forget by the time I reach home.

While I have always been involved with poetry, I do not think of myself as a poet although there are some people who do. I accept the idea that I picked up in France from the poet Loys Masson: While you are alive you may say quite correctly that you write poetry. But only after you are dead can you be called a poet. Or was it, much later, that Jacques Brel said this to me when we drank *alcool* in his apartment.

While I write poetry the reader can see by gaps in time (see dates) that I did not devote my total creative effort to poetry. The sirens of necessity pulled me away. The children never urged me into public relations nor into television, the landlord did. So, I made a living.

But no one can make a living writing poetry. That's what I like about it. Not so much that poetry is pure but rather that poetry is an act of free will which, if you believe religious people, is at the very core of the human condition.

Eric Blau

Brief Journey

International Publishers
1952

Among These Dead I Have Gone Counting
A Fragment of a Poem Which
Did Not Work

She sat cross-legged near the fountain
To count — one to ten — the ants she had
  discovered.
The courage came to reach down,
To lift one into the world
Among the trees and passing clouds.

The fountain flew from its stone;
The houses shuddered to powder.
The calm air, the constant friend
Took fright and pushed the world away
Leaving her unmarked and warm
And dead in my arms.

The sun, ungrieved rose to flood the square
And the moon, the blind cyclopic eye, passed
  over.
The earth sprawled over with the dead,
Said nothing, was ready to swallow all.
The wind came, an only mourner.

Among these dead I have gone counting.
And searching and fingering
And smelling and weeping
I can explain nothing away.

1944
Late in the Summer —
Inland from Normandy

Lajos of Koscord
For Alexander and Julia, my parents

My grandfather Lajos of Koscord
Died on an unknown day
Not with crowds like Joan of Arc
But like a leaf among leaves
Torn from the fields of Hungary
Where he burned.

He was an old man
His sons reared and scattered
On the earth. He died alone
He had been a Jew among Jews
His dust grows wheat on Hungary

Where he burned.

He was a Jew of Koscord
And a man of his land.
His nation continues him.
Each tree remembers him
He is not divided from Hungary
Where he burned.

1944

On Seeing Our Dead

My battle lines, at last, are formed.
Each bend, each jutting iron wedge
Is understood.

Terror falls away like dried mud.
The face of death changes:
There is no dark closing shadow
Swooping forever at the throat.
Dying, yes; but never death:

Dying as flowers die, crumbling gently
To make a higher earth for brighter blossoms.
I stand here where comrades lie.
I see ahead over the mounds
A life which is ours.

1944

What The Losses Are

I saw the house where first we loved
Before the wars came down.
I saw myself in the door's poor glass
Crashed there like a stone.

The landlord has never fixed the stair
Nor brought light into the hall.
The smell of wine from the cellar floor
Fades into the walls.

I saw the window of our old room
Before the blind came down.

I remembered us in the winter days
Shattered by the dawn.
O if other loves in other rooms
Expire with little cries
We will know what the losses are
Since we in love survive.

1943

The Paula March

Each gift I gave was sinister
The orange for Dudah
The clothes for Monique
The shoes for Paula.

(Beware of the boys with the cigarettes,
The boys with the chocolate bars.)

Gaudy was my packaged love
Yet paled so by your return.
I kissed you cheek on cheek with commodity
You burned my lips with your new liberty.

(Beware of the boys with the shining ships,
The boys with the steel guitars.)

13

I will never give you such gifts again
For each must take his own.

Dudah take the orange groves!
Monique take the mills!
Paula march all over France!

> 1945
> *Poesie*, Translated into
> the French by Paul Eluard

The Miners In The Exhibition Cases
For Pablo Neruda

> *On view at the Museum of Natural History*
> *in New York are the bodies of two ancient*
> *Chilean miners. They were presented to*
> *the museum in 1899 by J. P. Morgan on*
> *whose property, the Restadaura Mine, they*
> *had been discovered.*

In the showcases,
Lost among the mastodons,
Made green by the copper
Which buried them,

Lie two Chilean miners.
Among the careful echoes
Of heels clattering
Lie two early gifts
Of J. Pierpont Morgan.

An arm cropped off
At the elbow,
The tools out of reach,
The water bag dry,
The ore basket empty.
Black braided hair
On the faded Indian face,
Rough loin cloth
Between the stringy thighs,
The gay (unexplained)
Tasseled ankle bracelets.
There was a woman
Who waited hours
After he went under
The green tide of ore —
Centuries sealing over him
And J. Pierpont Morgan
Riding toward him
On a steamshovel
With glass cases

Under his arms.
She waited sensing her loss
Sweating between her breasts
Cold drops of loneliness.
But the miner was not coming.
J.P. Morgan was coming:
To Chile, to Atacama,
To all the continents
With glass cases
Under his arms.

Like the memory of hammers
Preceding the Conquistadors
And the advent of Anaconda
The guard goes tapping
Across the floors
Of J.P. Morgan's reliquary.

The green ore
Goes over J.P. Morgan
The centuries hover over him.
The miners ride toward him
On steam shovels
With glass cases
Under their arms.

No one is waiting
For J.P. Morgan

1943

The Seasons On Ninth Street

Did winter come and was it white?
And were we always cold beyond the heat
Beyond the glow of the burning iron stove?
When winter came with its badge of ice
We could not run away.
There was no south to warm our dreams,
No heated seas, no flying fish at play.
So in brigades we charged the streets
And like dragons we burned the air.
We turned our thoughts to eskimos
Mushing across their unstained snows.
We knew what we had to know:
It was so much colder there.
But not too much so. For this boy
Once stood on the freezing deck
Where blow by whistling blow he saw
The river wind toss the seagulls up

Where high and bright in the icy sun
They froze in time and memory. . . .

I remember when springtime came.
We listened hard for absent birds.
And from below the thawing stone
With such enormous ears we heard
The seeds of hope split their coats
And thrust the busted pavements up.
With these enormous eyes we bent the light
To brightly paint all the Ninth Street walls.
Oh, we sang a song for April
And we sang a song for May
And there was no day which was not rare
On Ninth Street or in Tompkins Square.
The cobblestones braved the iron wheels
Until the green grass arose
To make the stone wounds heal.
And then, and then, one day
A ragged red flower mysteriously appeared
And from the east and from the west
The thawing people came
And with profound hosannas pronounced:
A rose!

Summer has come!
Let all revolutions slumber now.
Let all warriors hide away their guns
For the invading sun has won the streets
With its soft cannon of sweat and lust.
When I saw the girls beneath their skirts
How I loved them each by each.
The name of manna was *Charlotte Russe*;
Celery Tonic was our wine.
To the cops we swore it was God
Who opened all the hydrants up
To wash down all the grimy skies.
Wawdeemeelow was a penny a slice
So we hung out our doubts to dry
All our rags were washed and pressed
And stick ball brought us fame.
We rejoiced ourselves for ninety days
Before October came.

Autumn is the softest chain
It links both ice and rose
It is the hot mirror of the cold to come
And the summertimes we've closed.
And regard the leaves!
How they all fall down!
Patina of green on doubloons of gold

The coins of God; the coins which buy
Our fast and fading times.
Autumn is the softest chain
Which links good life to death
The softest chain, the chain of gold
Which draws away the breath.

1949

Let Me Tell You About Moses

1972

On My First Visit to Israel

Bobbs Merrill

Let Me Tell You About Moses

Love, Let me tell you about Moses
About Moses and Me and the way it was.
Love, He was a Jew so long ago
When they put him in the stream to flow
Down the river, down, down, the river
Over the stones and mud and was it God
Or just Pharaoh's daughter,
    her hands in the water?
But someone else was floating and it was Me.
Caught in the bulrushes and lost and lost
In some future time.

Love, Let me tell you about Moses
About Moses and Me and the way it was.
Love, He was a Jew when God was new
When he stood with the women by the well
In Midian, down, down, in Midian
On that land where the hills skipped like lambs.
The water was cool down deep in the pool
Where someone else was watching and it was Me,
Standing at the roadside and lost and lost
In some future time.

23

Love, Let me tell you about Moses
About Moses and Me and the way it was.
Love, he was a Jew when Pharaoh played God
When the ten plagues came down in Egypt land
In Egypt land down, down in Egypt land
Where their lives trickled down into the sand
And with straw and mud they mixed their blood
But someone else was bleeding and it was Me
Standing at the roadside and lost and lost
In some future time.

But the Red Sea opened
And the Desert frowned
And Sinai reared up
And Moses climbed
And God came down
The mountain side
The bush it burned
The words were traced
Moses saw God's shoulder
But not God's face
And Moses came down
The mountain side,
Moses came down
The mountain side.

Love, Let me tell you about Moses
About Moses and Me and the way it was.
Love, He was a Jew as we all must be
When we set out in the stream to flow
Down the river down, down the river
Over the stones and mud looking for God
Finding Pharaoh's daughter —
soft hands in the water
And she knows that we are floating.
It's only us caught in the bulrushes,
Lost and lost in some future time.

Down the river.
Down, down
Down the river,
Down, down
In the bulrushes
Lost, lost
In some future time.

1972

Jerusalem

It is a market place,
Brass and lamb skins
And gates.
It is a market place,
Dates and beef sides
And cries.
It is a market place,
Open for business
Trading in Coca-Cola
And God.

It is a hustlers' place,
Life spilling from sacks
And gourds.
It is a hustlers' place,
Crying the glory
Of Thirty Cents.
It is a hustlers' place,
Selling memories
Lost beneath the flesh.
And the City,
Fouling its nest,
Growing over itself,
Replacing its walls

Like teeth
Becoming false,
Placing all Gods
Before me

Splitting one saviour
In two equal parts
Of bone and tears
Below the wooden ramp
Of the indoor Calvary
The metrodome of the ungraspable death. . . .

Barring another saviour
From the Golden Gate
With Turkish iron
And a lawn of graves
Brooding from Mount Olive
Looking across the orchards
Of the lucky, waiting, well-positioned dead. . . .

But the peddlers know it all
And you can get six-to-five pick 'em
On any God you call
And only their stalls are filled
With the Flesh, the Blood and the Holy Spirit
And everybody is waiting for Godot

Except the Arabs and the Jews and the Christians
Floating like miracles with gold teeth
In the squares of darkness
They call their own.

It is a market place
Rendered to Caesar and God
Those historic cruising cops
Who make their smiling rounds
Their shoulders brushing
All the narrow stations.

Elijah unrisen in the olive groves
Mohammed lost in the flames
And some bravos dragging Jesus
Out of Town
Because life must go on
And there are things to sell.

And a third saviour glowing
Beneath the Golden Dome
His steed of fire
Eating coals and pawing
His future flight

Across the skies
Of total redemption. . . .

1972

I Think I Told You Once
For Elly Stone, my wife, hearing her sing
in Tel Aviv for the soldiers of Israel

I think I told you once
I heard a bird sing
In a Scottish wood.
Just one bird
Caught in the mist
Which moved like ribbons
Through the dwarf trees.
It was alone. It was calling.
(That's what a song is. You know that.
Someone alone. Someone calling.)
The song came
In little bursts
Like a kid's whistle;
The wood bead spinning.
Then, as if all the winds converged,
The sound held,

29

Extended,
Spinning like glass and silver
Moving among those blind stubby arms
Of the almost naked trees
And I died because the song died.
I was a soldier then
In the comic rig
Of an indexible war.

I sought for my childhood
For the whistle hooked
To the sailor suit
Hung in the window of the past.
But I was looking the wrong way.
It was the self-conscious,
Unself-conscious eye of the soldier poet.
(A leaf! . . . the secret of life,
A tower! . . . The solitary finger in the dike of
    heaven,
A chestnut! . . . All the churches and urchins of
    Paris;
Wondering if Masson would understand
If gentle Eluard would smile. . . .)
But I was looking the wrong way.
It was your sound. It was you,
Alone and calling on the morning

Of a day which would not come
For a very long time.
When I first heard you sing. . . .
But you know now that the wood,
The mist and the bird came back;
I think I told you once.

1972

The Nation, The State, The Borders, The Old Opera

Perhaps we have come too late
Across the ocean sea
To the Nation State. It is all overgrown
With the lichen and fungi of dreams.
Yet no regrets, no sighs, no sorrows.
For in the twenty scattered centuries
Where we have wandered the nights were lit,
Not by lights of homes we never knew
But by the bone and blood of bondage
And by those throbbing lamps
    we have returned. . . .

But it is so small!
As small as all the places of childhood
Crammed stone by stone into the Testament.
Here Abraham dropped his knife.
Here Joshua stopped the night.
Here David. There Solomon.
Isaac, Aaron, Ruth, Moses.
The memories of manna,
The mountains worn down
And the rubble of the casual
Empty years and for all our yearning
That awful bad joke:
Where have you been lately?
And we are too weary to name
The ghettos which girdle the globe

We are home
And we must go greening the sands,
Putting up towers and teaching
The old land the new ways of milk and honey.
We fill the air with flowers,
Fix all the unhinged doors,
Brush the cobwebs from the caves.
And if it is not the storied glory of the Temple
It is at least the sweetness of the *shtetl*
In a summer without pogroms.

And it is all so exquisitely possible
That we quarrel. . . .
We are still a stiffnecked people.
Indestructible in tragedy,
Magnificent in war.
But, Oh, Delilah, Delilah!
The softness of Delilah
In the sweet beds of peace;
Orgasms preceding thunder,
Prologues of blindness and wrath!
Until the chained columns are struck,
Until we bleed, until we are crushed,
Until we are only our remarkable selves —
Stuck in the Talmud, Rashi and Gomorrah,
Stuck in the implied songs of the *chazanim*,
Stuck like the jawbones of asses,
In the crumbling fields of Ashkelon,
A dusty stage on the main drag
To anybody's destiny

So we face the sea and listen to the wind.
We shuffle down the grassy aisles
And think we hear the flautist at his reed
And perhaps the timpanist
Laying his sticks to the leaves.
We applaud, one-handed and echoing.

(A little bit of Zen, a little bit of *gevalt*).
It is an opera! It is an opera
Of prurient vintage but it must be played
Because we have the sets for it
And one tattered copy of the score
And all the parts and some of the musicians
And more players than we can use
And costumes which will not divide
Quite like loaves and fishes.
There to the West lies Jordan!
There, where the hills rise, *Syrie*!
There is the sea and there Egypt!
And the hills are alive with the sound of Philistines
And the arias are second-rate even if they are old
And at the top of our voice we sing
And at the end,
Behind the massed and bannered stage,
The sun rises.

We have been here before.
We have paid the price before,
Always at the scalper's rate,
Never a twofer, never a freebee,
Never, never a subscription seat!
Except this time we pay at the box
And there's room inside.

It is our very own opera!
At long last ours
Not someone else's road show!
(By the way, do you like opera?)
Our State, Our Nation singing
Even as all the States and Nations sing
And the borders, what about the borders,
The blood red lines of agony?
In appropriate pain
They will be set down.
Here, there, somewhere.
And, of course, they will not be right.
Yet once we did bring water out of a stone —
Which falls
Somewhere between magic and miracle.
That was very long ago.
This is not exactly an encore.
But we are on stage.

1972

Four Fantasies For A Very Old Shoemaker

1. *This Is The Center Of The World*

This is the center of the world.
This has always been so.
The sun always rises
In the Olive groves
And sets in the sea by the road.

This is the center of the world.
This has always been so.
The Lord always rests here
On the Sabbath night
And listens to men sing His song.

This is the center of the world.
This has always been so.
The wind always washes
The seas of the sky
It plants dreams of peace as it blows.

That's all my wisdom, my son, my son,
That's all I have to say.
A man who is born
At the center of the world
Can never go away.

That's all my treasure, my son, my son.
All this I leave to you.
The night and the morn
At the center of the world,
My dream already come true.

That's all my belief, my son, my son
All this I bequeath to you
A mighty nation at peace at last
This endless future, this endless past
To do what you're born to do.

For this is the center of the world
This has always been so
The sun always rises
In the olive groves
And sets in the sea by the road

This is the center of the world.
This has always been so.
The Lord always rests here
On the Sabbath night
And listens to men sing His song.

This is the center of the world.
This has always been so.

The wind always washes
The seas of the sky —
It plants dreams of peace as it blows.

2. Jonah Will Appear

Jonah will appear.
Seaweed in his hair.
He will smell of the sea.
He will stand right there.
— In the belly of the whale
My boots are gone.
I need new boots
Or I can't go on
To Jerusalem. . . .

Old Moses will come
With his tablet and rod.
He'll be proud and tall
As if he just faced God
— On Sinai, he'll say,
My sandals were torn.
I need new sandals
Or I can't go on
To Jerusalem. . . .

Solomon will arrive
As wise as can be,
The crown on his head
Resting uneasily.
— I can't think, he'll say,
For my feet ache so.
I need stout shoes
Or I cannot go
To Jerusalem. . . .

And Oh, Praise His Name,
The Messiah will sit here.
And Oh, Praise His Name
He will sit in my chair
And I will wash his feet
In a silver bowl.
I will make him sandals
Of burnished gold
Then we'll all go on
To Jerusalem. . . .

David will appear
His harp in his hand
And David will sing
Of the Promised Land

His voice is rich
But his soles are thin
— Please mend my boots
Or I can't go in
To Jerusalem. . . .

Joshua strides on.
The trumpets blare.
But there are no more wars
Raging anywhere
— Too many victories
Have burst these seams
I need new boots
To march to other dreams
Of Jerusalem. . . .

And, Oh, Praise His Name
The Messiah will smile
And Oh, Praise His Name.
He will call me His Child
And I will wash his feet
In a silver bowl
And I will make him sandals
Of burnished gold
And we will all go on

We will all go on
We will all go on
To Jerusalem

3. *The Organ Of Hazoreah*

In all the Universe, Oh Lord
On none of your kibbutzim
Could anywhere be found an organ
But one was made, Adonai Elohim,
And it was played at Hazoreah. . . .

In all the Universe, Oh Lord,
On none of your battleground
Could anywhere be found an organ
But one was made with a heavenly sound
And it was played at Hazoreah

In all the Universe, Oh Lord
On none of your Elysian Fields
Could anywhere be found an organ
But one was made and you can hear it peal
When it is played at Hazoreah

4. *Where Are The Angels?*

I see Your great rivers flow
I see Your round moon aglow

I see Your fields of wonder grow
In the path of Your Great Hand.
I hear Your deeps and oceans roar
I see Your winged creatures soar
I hear Your Name in song adored,
Dear Lord, in every hymn
But where are the seraphs,
Where are the angels,
Where are the cherubim?

I see Your great cities rise
I see Your temples fill the skies
And, lo, Your armies multiply
In the path of Your Great Hand.
I see Your great orb of gold
I see Your Universe unfold
I hear Your name in song adored,
Dear Lord, in every hymn
But where are the seraphs,
Where are the angels,
Where are the cherubim?

For A Bedouin Girl Of Twelve
Who Got Married The Year Before

When I looked to the South
(After you had taken the candy)
It was to look for a ball
Or a bicycle or some sign of childhood.
It was not to turn away from you.
I wanted to say: The desert would be
A funny place filled with wheels
Although self-propelled red
And yellow balls would do
Rolling over lifts and dips in the sand
Or bowling from tree to tree
On the scraggly oasis
Where the growling camel suddenly pissed
Straight down.
It was not to turn away from you.
I wanted to say: I'm not really a tourist.
But I could see myself etched on your eyes
And I confessed it to myself,
Just as I confessed that you were not a child
Although there were no breasts
Lifting against the burlap wrap
Which embraced you
Against the rare rain which fell

I wanted to say: Who is your man?
Who paid your father's price?
Who took you into his bed at night
And did he gently find the way?
But that would have been prying.

I wanted to say: I hope you don't get
Knocked up until you're twenty
Because everything is leather
And downhill after that.
I wanted to say something obvious:
Like why don't you cut out,
Why don't you run? There must be
A better oasis than this one.
But you were smiling and scratched your ass
And I gave you the rest of the candy.

And The Colonel's Wife Said . . .

Let's not make love tonight, Dov
You are unclean and you should sleep
Outside the room, outside the city
With the other men who have their time
Who are letting blood.

You are just returned from Lebanon.
You are unclean and you should sleep
Outside the room, outside the city.
The desert wind will dress the wounds
Which death has made.

Let's not make love tonight, Dov
You smell of death and liberation
If you touch my breasts, open my thighs,
I will look away and turn to salt
Although I love you.

Dov, Dov, if you trust the night
Go quickly into the darkness
And I will say three prayers:
That you will rise up at day,
That they shall forgive you,
That you shall forgive them.

An Interview With A Southern Ape
Confined With The Asian Flu
To An Old Essene Cave

Of course, I am astounded to find you alive and
well and living at the Dead Sea.

I'm sick. I'm going to die.

It's only a bad cold; it will pass.

*From your mouth to God's ears. Did you drink the
water down there? It's awful.*

It's unpotable; but there's a fresh water stream
running into it.

I stay clear of that. Lots of brush.

There are no lions, no predators.

Where did they go?

Who?

The lions, the lions!

I don't know, really. They haven't been in these
parts for centuries.

46

That's when they get you. Clever, clever,
    those lions.

But you? Have you got a name? What are you
    doing here? Nobody has seen you around
    in twenty million years.

What the hell are you talking about?

It doesn't matter. What is your name?

You're getting obscure.

Your name — what do they call you?

What kind of shit is that? I'm a Southern Ape.
    Australopithecus. I look around if someone
    grunts. If it's a broad, I look around
    quicker. I had a femur bone here. Did you
    see it?

No.

It was a helluva femur bone. Zok! Take out a
    full-grown baboon just like that. Also my
    antelope jaw. Good one. Sharp as a
    sonuvabitch. Hate to be here with a bad
    cold and no weapons. You sure there are
    no lions down at the stream?

Quite sure.

Things are different than they used to be.
No lions?

None. Not one.

Hmmmm. So what else is new?

Israel. A new state. A new nation.

Herbivorous or carnivorous?

You don't understand. A state. A nation. The
first Jewish State in two thousand years.

Not something you eat? Not something that eats
you?

No, no. It's a group of people — Jews who have
returned here to live.

A troop of apes?

No. No. People. Jewish people like me.

Well, you're an ape of a sort as far as I can see.

Have it that way if you will. People or apes, we
have all gathered here in one place to live.

Aha, you have your own territory!

That's right.

Then somebody must be attacking it.

How did you know that?

*After a few million years you get to know things.
Once you establish territory it gets all the
other apes uptight. They simply have got
to attack. You know, the territory is always
greener on the other side. . . .*

Amazing.

And who are you attacking?

Well, we are having certain difficulties with Egypt,
Lebanon, Jordan and the Palestinian
guerrillas. . . .

*Don't take it too seriously. In the end it always
works out. The big problem, the really big
problem, is the pecking order. You can win*

49

*all the wars but that only means you sit
around the water hole and throw mud at
each other. Somebody always wants to be
the Big Ape. Then the Deputy Big Apes
always want to beat up on the Nothing Apes
and eat all the prime antelope cuts and also
get the best looking chicks.*

I take it that you are not the Big Ape.

*And not a Deputy either. And if you must know
the truth, I've got lots of lumps on my head.
When it comes to eating, it's always antelope giblets. And I can't look at the crotch
of a tree without getting horny. . . .*

Why don't you leave here? Come down with me
and I'll show you the country.

*No thanks. Last time I went down I saw those
skinny apes writing funny things on round
paper. Nuts . . .*

Did you talk to them?

*I tried but after a couple of head swoks I said to
hell with it. Then I got this cold.*

Come out and sit in the sun. You'll get better. The
cold will disappear.

No *thanks. All I have left is this cold and if I lose
that what will be the meaning of life?*

Having a cold cannot be the meaning of life. Is
that all you have learned in twenty million
years?

No.

Well, what have you learned?

*That a cold is psychosomatic and the worst thing
is not to have a normal sex life.*

Is that all? What about Nations? What about
God? What about the Destiny of Man?

What the hell are you talking about?

Bigger issues.

*Bigger issues are lions. And, any ape who goes
around saying, "There are no lions," doesn't know
his ass from his femur bone. . . .*

51

Who Is A Jew?

I say Tom McGrath is a Jew
And he will not dare deny it.
I cannot speak for his father
Lost on the north forty in Dakota.
I cannot speak for his mother
Who may yet light candles to Mary.
I am only sure of McGrath
Because of the quality of his tears.

I say Rigo Jancsi is a Jew
And he cannot ever deny it
Because he was a Gypsy fiddler
Who died unknown in New York
Widowing a Hungarian Countess.
What's left is some pastry bearing his name:
My father told me this when I was small
So Rigo must be a Jew after all.

I say that I am a Jew
And I never knew how to deny it.
I know it as well as I know God
Or as well as I do not know God
Or almost as well as the Rabbis know God.

You must remember me.
I came from Ninth Street,

The Upper Ghetto to the North
Where all that was asked of a Jew
Was to survive. *Henaini!*
Here I am after all these years
Still saying it, still insisting,
Not waiting for the Great I Am
Or for Our Teacher or for Our Tormentor
Just being it, just Zenning it.
I say I am a Jew
Who is fool enough to deny it?

The Wall

I touched it and I tried to remember
A prayer; even the one for bread.
But nothing was there on my tongue
Or in my head where a thousand walls
I had built and broken
Lay in the ruins of personal time.
I listened to the voices rising up
Running among the cracks
Horizontal and vertical tears,
The heavenward thrust
Of brown and yellow beards
And the embarrassed paratrooper
Cutting the granite words

53

From his fragile page
God is One. There is only One God.
And for me?
You will remember
I did not cry
Or speak
Or bend
And no one judged me
Nor even looked to check.
For the Wall that Solomon left
Was also for those of us
Whose lips do not erode the rock
Yet who carry in their mason's hands
The pity and the passion of every stone
To build new temples from the dust . . . .

A Primer For Jews, Non-Jews And Others

1.

The Yemenites take four wives
They've done it all their lives
But the Talmud is filled with laws
And each one is a holy cause
Yet the Yemenites are not in sin
Since there's precedent therein
On this score the judges may not be tough
Since four wives, they say, is punishment enough

2.

In Jerusalem you cannot kid a Jew
If it isn't very old
Then it's very very new

3.

That's how it was with the Crusaders
They caught you now and screwed you later
Thus if you carefully look around
Some Arabs are dark and some are blound

4.

The Druzes aren't Arabs
The Druzes aren't Jews
They live in little houses
Which have enormous views

5.

At the Hilton in Tel Aviv
People find it hard to live
Not because the food is rotten
Things like that can be forgotten
In the Holy Land one profoundly regrets
That God can be charged American Express

6.

There was a little boy from Haifa
Who really couldn't be nicer
When told Israel was antique
Much of it Roman much of it Greek
He accepted the news, his eyes on his shoes
And continued to piss in the creek.

Ghandi's* Party

I went to Ghandi's goddam party
And everyone was there
No one knew when the party started
And nobody seemed to care
We played on flutes and tambourines
We pounded little drums
No one knew why we celebrated
And rumtitumtita tum.
I went to Ghandhi's goddam party
And it was a hell of a thing!
We got high on Carmel brandy
And every Jew can sing,
And every Jew can sing!

Ho la dah didah
Ho lah didid dah
dah dah dah

I went to Ghandhi's goddam party
Where we got drunk with dreams.
No one knew when the dreams got started,
It was long ago it seemed.
We played on flutes and tambourines,
We pounded little drums

No one knew why we celebrated
And rumtitumtitatum

* Ghandhi was the nickname of one of Israel's
leading generals at that time.

For My Tribesmen On The New Left,
The Old Right And The Dead Center

Poor, poor me, out of Abraham, out of Jacob
All American yet well circumcised
With an ear to Paine's drum
With an ear to David's harp
And where in Mao or Marx
Or in Mein Kampf
Or in the Talmud
Am I defined?
You will not find me
Among the closet Jews of Cairo
Or Moscow or Washington
Or six-pointed and peaceful
In the synagogues.
I am a Jew
Just a plain Jew
Out of Alexander of Koscord
Out of Julia of Golacs

And going back and back and back
Among the begats without pride
But with so much anger
Because it is still true
That I must show my card to fools
And sew my yellow star upon my sleeve.
Or is it only in a dream that we embrace?
In night images occupying sense
From border to border;
Bodies which have no weight, no smells,
Which move in motions too slow or too fast
Over flat maps which designate no roads,
No towns, no tomorrows?
And do we not awake
Each of us alone
In the cold pre-National Halls of Mirrors?
You crying: I love my enemy more than myself. . .
You crying: I love myself more than my enemy . . .
You whimpering: Be still, be still,
For my sake, be still. . . .

Reflections. Left-handed statements of light
Bounced once to the eye
To the inner eye
To the dream
Where we embrace in the world we cannot touch

I am, I feel, I am as much as a homing salmon
I am, I feel, I am no less than a turtle
    flopping to the sea
I am, I feel, I am no less than lots of
    monkeys sucking for the treetop air of home
Yet I do not know where I live.

And what does it all mean?
But that I believe that I am
That I was
That I will be
That I will not be
That I will be again
Or that I will be nothing
If I am not a Jew.

When there was no Israel
I did not need it
And when there was an Israel
I could not surrender it.

About The Mount Of Olives And
The Great Atlantic And Pacific Tea
Company

Poppa, when I saw the Mount of Olives
I thought of you and I thought of Momma
And not for a moment was I bitter
Although being bitter comes easily to heart
But the blood pumps and the bile thins out in the
    stream.

For what are they but graves
Rolling down to the gates and the walls,
Jews lying under the green,
Box seats on the fifty-yard line,
Clean view of the Messiah when he comes. . .

But Jews lie under every earth
And, God only knows, on how many hills
As you lie on your Mount Moriah
Not that one on which Solomon built
But one of those other Moriahs
Which rise up on old potato fields
Or on bumpy plots the builders left behind
Which somehow fill the bill
For even in these foreign places
Ancient names are magical.

On the top of the Mount of Olives, Poppa,
The winter breeze is cool
And the tourists play at eternity
And reach up to God as they look down
And it would be good (for them)
Except for the Arab kids clustered
Around the cars with hands full
Of holiness at about a dime a feel.
They have such sweet faces and sell us
Fortune and good luck and know
That weeping Jews are suckers
And the softest marks to touch. . . .

Over at your place in New Jersey, Poppa,
The ivy in two shades of green
Sends its roots deeply down
To blanket you against the snows
And Momma waits to take her place
Alongside, beneath the monument.
I don't think she thinks of Mount Olive.
It is this place which is nearest heaven
And nearest peace and nearest you.

I suppose that I am satisfied, too,
Although I resent the hard left turn
Off the highway and through the painted gate
To see our name cut into the stone.

The name looks fine, clean and deep,
But I see it and I think
The whole thing is so obscene.

All that way from Koscord,
All those years behind the wheel
Of how many yellow taxicabs
Only to be planted here.
Not below the Temple Wall
Not even beneath Omar's Mosque
But beneath the brand of the A&P
Which sits on the hill above
Smiling down in great red thrusts.
Shit, Pop, hasn't it always been
That way for us?

Ah, Ahmad . . .

Hey, Ahmad, this is history
History seen off a high
Through a haze of smuggled hash.
Glorious giggling in Gomorrah,
Naked with Nefertiti on the Nile,
Then hung over with rage.
Hey, Ahmad, don't cut your leg off
With that wild M-1 scimitar
Just give me your soul-felt
Estimate of the fucking miserable dirty Jews
While I kip up and cut you
With my run at the fucking miserable dirty Arabs
Hey, Ahmad, look how they spread out
Like camel dung across the desert
Brown on brown —
Star worshipers, God worshipers
Word worshipers, cat worshipers
Let's all climb the mountain
And vomit en ensemble. . . .
Don't hog it; pass it.
I am thinking about
Mount Quarantel
My eyes focusing

On the tuna can
Dropped in the sand
Now you be a good gook
Pass the pipe
Before Christ
Crawls out . . . .

Hey, Ahmad, what think you of yonder moon
That pale and glowing orb
Which God Himself hath placed?
Hey, Ahmad, it is filled with plastic flags
Red stains and iron bugs
Beeping all the time
Yet, by my troth, it has much to do
With our tides!
I dig the calligraphy in the Koran
Flat out it beats the marks in the Torah . . .

Hey, Ahmad, you are playing the part
Of the National Liberationist
And me, poor fellow,
Must repeat the lines of the imperialist
Depending, you know,
If the casting director comes
From Moscow and is pure Stanislavsky
Or, lack a day, the producer,

A method man, from the Pentagon
Streamlined and mumbling:
Lay it on, MacDuff . . . .

Pass the pipe, baby,
This is the destiny bag.
Whose father's ghost
Goes there among the dunes?

Hey, Ahmad, it is the numbers game
With the sixes and nines gone straight.
Hey, Ahmad, it is the numbers game
With the eights jammed up the ass of a corpse.
Hey, Ahmad, we are three million killer Jews
Carpeted from sea to sea like locusts
And we will shofar up ten million more
Just in case, in the end, you will wipe us out.
(I really think that would be unfortunate
But at least you will have broken the old record.)
Hey, Ahmad, don't shed a tear for us
(Protocols of the Elders of Zion; kikes, you know.)
Hey, Ahmad, we know how to die
We're professionals
And quite good at it
Torquemada was a shit kicker.

And here you come!
Two hundred, three hundred million Arabs
Lead by the son of Arafat
And Lorenz of Arabia
(Turn your throat up, old wolf!)
Over the hills and through the valleys
Yowling: ZAP, POW, BAM, SPLAT and PIFF
We are dead.
Will you bury us?
Where will you bury us?

Ah, Ahmad, what do you think
When you think of that holocaust?
Could it go the other way?
Could it be us tearing you up?
The equation doesn't reverse.
The Hashemite King will kill more Palestine kids
Than all the Jew Battalions.
The Cadillac Sheiks will suck more Arab blood
Into the pipes of thick oblivion
And the newly minted socialists will say the words
Which I have kissed
And leave you with the tuna cans.
Ah, Ahmad, Power eats people
And Arabs taste as good as Jews . . .

Ah, Ahmad, what a night is this night
We could walk along the sea road
Picking dates and figs and feeling good
We could be the Middle East
And Juliette could be the sun
And if she were your sister
I would sleep with her
If you understand that this is love.

The Journey Not Yet Winding Down
1932
For Adolph William Schwimmer,
my cousin

In that summer we were young enough
To see the swans on English ponds
And the jungles where Tarzan flew
In special trees; but we secretly knew
That he was Lord Greystoke and impervious
To the dangers stalking post-pubic Jews
In Bridgeport.

In that summer we were young enough
To see the stars in unwrapped skies

And mark them out and claim them all for us,
Our skins tightening, for we secretly knew
That the vastness of heaven was cold to the feel
Its hard edge fused to our passing dreams
On Poplar Street.
In that summer we were young enough
To know that we were to be thrown like dice
Or Odysseus into a diaspora far wider
Than from here to California and that we would go
In white hearses and gray ships to places
Where we were mechanics or fools, doing our
    thing,
Moving on.

1945 Paris
So next we meet in Paris
Underneath the Arch
Standing firmly on the tomb
Of the Unknown Soldier.
(That was Pappa's war)
And your pocket got picked.
And I wept for France
(Ma patrie, ma belle, mon amour!)
Oh, the shame, oh, the woe,
That your wallet could be lifted

Beneath the flooding tricolor
And the crosses of Lorraine
(Tant pis!)
So we tool around the town of Paris
In a G.I. half-ton truck
And note the Notre Dame
And celebrate our luck.
We never mention the Camps at all
The row on row of bony Jews
The furnace flues did not suck up.
Our nostrils twitch on that air
For forever in the floating dust
Our shit-out-of-luck brothers are there.

The numbers are not tallied yet
And we are already numbed.
So we talk about the Tuileries
And go down to the old Marais
To find the first delicatessen
Which had opened up for trade
And try our rusty Yiddish
In halting household phrase.
You will be gone soon
In your flying machine.
I will go home by boat.
And in the slide of the coming years
We will meet in the graveyards
Where we put our *meshpocheh*

Down into the earth
And wash our hands and softly talk,
Caressing the kinescopes of childhood,
Knowing even as we walk on Main Street,
Bridgeport no longer exists

1971 Tel Aviv
So we meet again in Tel Aviv.
You are the same
And you are kind enough
To say I haven't changed.
Have I not, now?
And haven't you?
Me? I have kept all these years
To my strange belief in words;
Putting them down, putting them down
Into their own peculiar earth
And waiting too often for an arena
To spring up bravoing,
Saying my name in praise.
But I reap mainly wind and weeds.
Something finally grows but too late.
But I am so engaged and go on and hope
To do a few things well

And more and more I long to sit and feel the
    sun . . .
But you are surrounded by Israel
By the oranges and the mountains
By the ruins and by the sea
And you have planted marvelous vineyards.
And, yes, yes, of course,
You are still the old mechanic
And you have put together
Thousands of guns
Thousands of planes
Thousands of hard things
But you are the same
A patina of grease, still on your hands.
You are careful still
To rub your nose
With the back of your wrist
Your head is in your secret workshop,
So far away from the weeping market place.
You are the same.
I have not changed.
We play the game
We have not arranged.
Your hands are filled with birds.
You have built a nation.
My head is filled with words
Perhaps a song or two.

We part now and exchange gifts
You have given me Israel
And I have given you this . . . .

The Marsh Birds

The Fire Island Poems – 1986

1. These Birds, Ducks Rose Up

These birds, ducks, rose up
From the marsh. Then black birds.
My heart flew up,
Fell without soaring.
I am from the city.
Birds startle me. Frighten me.
Too close to my urban face.
They flap and rattle.
I am in the sun;
Too close to the marsh
In a chair of plastic bands.
I do not know these birds.
They are brightly anonymous.
No names. All birds are
Nameless yet designated:
The Robin of Childhood,
The Blue Bird of Happiness,
The Sea Gull of Hunger
Hovering over the River
Of the stone blind city
Alive, flapping forever
In my memory.
All other birds,
If there are other birds,
Are stuffed.

They neither sit nor fly.
Inside great or small museums
Where children in coupled queues
Go. Once.
Go once to mark
What they do not see:
The violent flight
Inside the seasonless kiosks
Of glass which does not reflect
Or reveal
They see a shadow,
And beneath that shade
Some red. A sun dying?
The more the shadow is black
The more the red is red.
Who hides there?

It is not the shadow
Of the dead owl.
It is not the flat dark
Of the murdered eagle
Whose poisoned wings
And choked cries divide
The absent air.
It is a shadow cast
By no form
On a ground touched
By no light.

It is black.
It is black, black. Black.

It is a shadow
With awful dimensions.
It has a thickness.
The thickness of many
Millions of shadows
Which can not cover
The press of rose
Which pierces that flat night
Without a thorn.
Some one is hiding in this shadow.
Who is under this darkness?

2. Bird, Anonyme, Grips The Reed

Bird, anonyme, grips the reed.
The reed so frail
It can not bear a cloud
Or butterfly
But what does the nameless bird
Know of this? It clutches
The stem in circling claws
Sways and slaps the air
With red lined wings.
My plastic banded chair squeaks.
The blackbird stares, rattles.
The reed rattles.

The universal marsh rattles.
Only the shadow does not rattle.
It ripples.
Wind brushes the water.
Colors, random leaves, fall, vanish.
Hinted vermillion holding no time,
Vanishes.

3. Now The Night. Now The Moon

Now the night. Now the moon.
Much like the perished sun.
Yellow. Heavy metal red.
It lays a way of light
Across the clam filled bay.
Pierces itself silently
On the spearing reeds.
Wounded light which does not bleed.
Can this moonlight
Drive these reeds to rune?
Or to music? Or to dance?
Moonlight is a ghost light
Passing through the wall of night
Moaning, groaning, rattling chains
Of empty deserted machines.
Do these rust?
Does a thousand year rain
Fill the sole and heel
Of the forgotten Giant Step?

Ducks float. Ripples burrow
Into their breasts and emerge
In new gold ridged trails.
The black birds are nowhere
Unless in secret places.
Secret places of red.
Secret places of black.
They have gone off.
Where? With whom?
Down, perhaps, with the drowned light
Where the sea grass roots grip
The tentative chaos where worms work.
Does God consider this bottom?
Was the world finished long ago?

4. Beyond The Marsh The Pleasure Boats

Beyond the marsh the pleasure boats
Sail the shallow sea.
The birds on reeds look toward the shore
And call to distances unexplored;
Call in wide tongues unknown to me.
The man from the Great City
Looks beyond the pleasure boats
Across the shallow sea,
Remembers the songs of marsh birds
Who have never leaped
The knuckled air of the Great City
Nor have ever sung

Its beginning nor its end.
My remembering eye falls
Into the palm of my hand.
I see the shadow.
It slips from my fingers
And falls,
Black and rose
And rose and black,
Without a splash.

5. *It Is Only A Marsh*

It is only a marsh,
Said the man from Missouri.
On both sides of my Big River
We are lousy with marshes
There are birds alright
And ducks like here.
That's a mallard there;
See it coming in heavy assed
Between those broken rushes
And that old rope net?
Listen, marshes are alright
If it's marshes you like.
But what is a marsh
Compared to the Ocean?
I come here by plane
Once every two, three years.
More often if I can, you know,

To see this great Atlantic.
That is an awesome phenomenon
No mortal man can comprehend.
So vast it can be measured
Only by itself or by an eye
Hanging out in space.
The sound of it! The strength of it!
The curling ceaseless terror
That grinds stones and ships
Into sand, almost soft, you know.
No marsh, no way, is that!
Obvious, ain't it?
A marsh is made in minutes
Of cosmic history. Rivers piss out
Little marshes as they stream.
Oceans, with cold contempt,
Spit out little marshes
By the millions. Spit them out
Filled with little lives
Thick with coexistences!
The Ocean, oh man, the Ocean!
See it! See that part of itself
Which reveals a vastness which swallows
All Leviathans!
A marsh is nothing.
An Ocean is almost God.
No blasphemy intended,
Said the man from Missouri.

It's just I feel so strong
About this awesome sea.
He hawked up a gob and spit
Powerfully over the deck rail
Nailing the stalk of a reed
Which bent deeply.
The black bird, gripping the reed
As it bowed, lifted its wings
And climbed into the air
As the reed rose up trembling.

6. Did A Storm Pass In The Night?

Did a storm pass in the night?
Did the thunder roll
Out of China 'cross the bay?
Did the gods of Gilgamesh
Fill the marsh with silver spears?
Was that the crash of rain?
Did the jagged light come
From slow swirling chaos?
Did the black birds shield their eyes
Behind soft mailed wings?
Were there cries?
Did the birds dive
Into secret dark bunkers?
Did the storm pass in the night?
Was there the crash of rain?
I was asleep in the narrow bed.

I awoke with the smell
Of the deluge now passed —
Distant soldiers mounted
On dark and distant clouds
Slipping over heaven's edge
Raw with pink scars of dawn.
One voice. Two voices. Three Voices.
Reeds bend under feathered weights.
Green ducks sail.
A white heron swoops down.
Was there a night?
Did I sleep in it?
Did a storm pass?

7. You Are Quite Incorrect, Said The Old Lady

You are quite incorrect, said the old lady
Holding the brim of her dark straw hat
Against a momentarily expected wind.
Summer people think this is a salt marsh.
But the bay does not enter into it!
Not at all! said the old lady.
It is wholly the work of the Water Company.
(She smiles dangerously across her dentures.)
You see, said the old lady,
The President thought a marsh would be nice.
When he ordered it and had it built
In less than six days
He said he felt somewhat like God.

Then the blackbirds found it;
Then the ducks, some swifts and muskrats.
They are after all, poor dears, true believers
And the marsh is surely their Eden
And the President surely is God
Or surely fulfills that function
Although the President will be the first
To admit that the marsh is far from perfect.
You will find no fingerling fish swimming
Nor tiny crabs which can rest on a penny.
There are too many mosquitos.
There is too little mystery,
Don't you know?
Although sometimes in the bright sun
You see a shadow which does not belong
And that is very strange.

8. Before The Marsh And to the Side

Before the marsh and to the side
Of the wooden slatted road
The Beach Rose grows.
It has a four petalled pink head
And makes me think of an anarchist.
A girl, that is, who once I loved
Down there in the Village.
She stopped Time as it ticked
By cutting her hair quite short
And lighting her cigarette at the end

Of her silver tipped smoking stick
And tying down her ample tits
Although the Twenties were long ago gone
And the War outside her window
Was perhaps a minute away.
She had a four petalled pink head.
She wanted to stop Time very much.
Perhaps she did.
For now I remember the anarchy
Filled with dunes and winds and a music
Neither of us could play.

9. The Night Talkers On The Radio

The night talkers on the radio
Ride on secret waves and tides
Knocking at the windows
And crying at the locks
Are the lovers in their beds
For now it's twelve o'clock!
Talkers.
Talkers to the marsh birds
Talkers to the bay waves
Talkers to warps, woofs and grids
Talkers to white dwarfs and black holes
Of a possible universe.
In your opinion, Dr. Queller,
What was the greatest of all loves?

On earth or in heaven?

Considering the time we have
on the air, why don't we stick to the earth
tonight. Heaven can wait. (heh! heh! heh!)

Yes. Well, Mr. Blue . . . .

Call me Barry. I'll call you Joyce.

*Doctor, I'd rather you called
me Doctor, Barry.*

OK. My guest is Dr. Joyce Queller.
The question is: What was the greatest of all
Loves? In your opinion.

*Well, Barry Blue, if I wanted to
play it safe I could say Samson and Delilah,
Romeo and Juliet, Petrarch and Laura, Tristan and
Isolde and so forth and so on. But what do we
really know about them as lovers or even people.
Was there a therapist?*

I see your point, doctor. It is a good point.

Thank you, Barry Blue. We must
fasten our minds on such more familiar lovers
As Frankie and Johnnie, Liz and Richard,
Joe and Marilyn, Maggie and Jiggs and so on
and so forth.

We will take a break here for some
Important Messages. Then we will return to
Dr. Joyce Queller and her latest best seller
The Lives And Loves of Maggie And Jiggs.

Talkers. Night Talkers.

. . . the most democratic of all
The Late Night Talk Shows. I want views
from all sides. This is Larry True. My guest
is Dr. Bedford Weller who put together the
Big One against all odds and obstacles.
Dr. Weller this is a great honor for me.

I am also honored.

Dr. Weller, you are my guest tonight,
Tell us, in your opinion, what are the various
advantages and disadvantages of, you know
what I mean, well, of NUCLEAR WAR?

Well, Larry, may I call you Larry?

Yes, call me Larry.

Talkers. Night Talkers.

Good evening. That was the latest
news. This is Cary Koo. This is the second
Hour of my interview with Mortimer Gettyfeller.
Let's talk about freedom. What does freedom
mean to you, Mr. Gettyfeller?

*Cary, if I may call you Cary, to me Freedom is the
Big F. To me Freedom is the God given right to
make money, the Big M.
Freedom, the Big F, is the right to get Rich,
The Big R.
An old corn pone guy with fried chicken did it.
Larry Flynt — With a few twists and kicks with
Porno did it.
From door to door with American Flags
Amway did it.
Very often even by strangers
I am asked, Gettyfeller how did you did it?*

And what do you answer, Mr. Gettyfeller?

The truth, Cary. It is God's work.
There is no way to get the Big M
Which leads to the Big R
Resulting in the Big F
Without the will
of the Big G. Pray with me, Cary.

Do we have to kneel?

No, I often do it standing up.

The Night Talkers talk.
The birds sleep.
The shining duck waits
For the morning or the apocolpyse.
The white heron conceives of the Big F.
It is a field beetle
Or a small mackerel.

10. Spontaneously Born The White Heron Sails

Spontaneously born the white heron sails
The still marsh waters of the morning
After the silver speared rain. White.
In the presence of the heron
The black birds fall silent.
The deep rose tinted shadow
Follows her among the reeds.

The heron finds me in my chair
Caring little to find me there
Or caring not at all
Except to suggest my smile.
Oh, she is the woman of memory
Perfectly preserved in the white amber
Of a July, a half century before
so clear, so clear!
Silk dress of white,
White Italian straw
Over golden hair
Which tress by tress
I swear was white!
I saw her from my secret place
Lift her endless legs of white
Gliding across the cobblestones
Stopping once to smile; *at me!*
How I adored you, oh, Heron!

11. In The Chair, First Coffee In Hand
In the chair, first coffee in hand
I dream the dreams of morning.
Behind my eyes something stirs.
In the marsh something stirs.
Ships in their tidy slips stir.
I stir. The coffee is stirred by me.
Out of the sea, of a sudden,
Came a House. A monster rising

Against the forming day.
Grey, cold, wingless it rolls
Over the smooth bay waves
Toward the calmness of the marsh.
Distantly I hear its monster voice.
It is groaning and creaking.
It is filled with motors.
It is remorseless as a remora
Sucking tight to the helpless barge.
It is a weathered house
With one eye cut
Into the middle of its forehead.
It is fronting the marsh.
It is pushing the sea before it.
Awake I stand, cup in hand,
Wondering what has God wrought?
The black birds rattle.
The reeds rattle.
The great monster with lateral scales
Brooding, breathing softly, not rattling,
Waits.

The monster's shadow
Without weight falls
Across the accepting marsh.
The fallen shadow is accepted
But the one eyed house

Can not be seen by the marsh.
It is too enormous to be seen.

12.

> Pilings Are Plunged Into The Earth Between
> The Marsh And The Bay. The House Is
> Rolled Off The Barge And Is Set On The
> Pilings. The House Is Established In The
> New Found Land By The Grants, Deeds
> And Special Laws Of The Town Selectmen
> Across The Bay.

And I dreamed buzzards and vultures
Flapped down and sat on the flat sunken roof
Shifting from claw to claw
Opening steel stayed wings
Waiting for the marsh to perish.
And I dreamed the black birds
Rose up like God's avenging angels
And in their numbers darkened the sky
High above the great shadow.
And in their crying numbers
They dropped down white acid missiles.
Marked and wounded the buzzards
And vultures lifted their wings
Cursed the angels and fell upward
Into the sun.
But in my dream the stained house

Riveted its shadow still and stood.
The One Eyed House will not be moved.
In my dream I sipped my coffee and I said:
It does not belong here. And I said:
It belongs here surely. And I thought:
All contradictions are made of wood
All angels right, all misunderstood.
In my dream the President of the Water Company
Wept for his lost magic pipe
Which had pissed out this marshy life
And in my dream the President said
He wants all to be saved.
In my dream I see the birds
And beer cans pray.
The shadow of the house stays.
Its dark teeth eat the reeds,
The birds, this scummy inland sea.
In my dream I see the Other Shadow.
It has not been eaten.

13. In My Dream I Undressed

In my dream I undressed
And went naked into the marsh.
My balls cold and small
There I was not heavier than the shadow
    or the light.
Into the cool water of the swamp
I reached down and scooped up

The mud and painted my body black.
I planted myself like a reed.
I danced quietly in a wind
Until the dawn came, until the sun rose
Above the boats, the barge,
And the one eyed house.
I was dry and grey and caked,
Bold cracklings carved on my flesh.
In my dream
In the dancing night among the reeds
Another Painter had come upon me.
In the dark mirror of the marsh
I saw a broad white band on my brow.
I saw the yellow circles around my breasts.
I saw the pearl green sheen
Of the mallard's neck upon my thighs.
On my shoulders I saw the bright red
Paint of the blackbird's wings.
I raised my arms and flew
High into the air and dived
With what unnamed joy!
Onto a single bending reed
And I held it in my claws
And screamed.
And in midair I mounted you
And knew I had done a mystery
Inside you a start of new feathered worlds.
I drove my father from the marsh.

I drove my son from the marsh.
I heard the last of a night music
Which had escaped the darkness
And was in the sun
And in my dream I knew
I myself was of the substance
Of a rose tinted shadow.

14. *There Are No More Marsh Birds*

There are no more marsh birds;
Nor duck nor heron nor swift.
I am in the Big City
Trying to remember
By what winds I have here arrived.
My skin is uncaked and uncolored.
There are no more marsh birds.
I am in the Big City
Among the rentable ruins
Trying to conjure up
By what magic I had flown
Back and down into the still waters
And into the deep fine silt.
Will I remember long
The rattle of the marsh?
Yes. But not purely.
For in a final wind
Tapping out a hollow beat

On a lonely *HighLife* can.
I wonder: Who put that there?
God is the answer.
Or, perhaps, the President
Who thinks, in a way, he is God.
What is important is the question.
I ask it now.
What is a marsh? Are there birds in it?

Talking to Myself as I Walk DownTown Along Broadway In the Morning

Random pieces (1989–1998)

1. What Was It Long Ago?
What was it? The sound?
Yes, the sound,
Echoing from the image.
Was it the image then?
Yes, the image.
But before that, what?
The biology of time, perhaps.
All of that.
Picking its way
Through the boy
Who will never know
If he found the poem
Or if the poem found him.

2. Talk Cheap Talk
Talk.
Cheap talk.
All day talk.
All night talk.
Talk is cheap.
Talk is money.
He must have this talk
And she, too, must listen.
They are a family

Although
The children, giggling, don't listen.
They are too young to know
That there is a God, that there isn't a God,
That six hundred million dead Afro-Americans
Created the world as we know it,
That the Jews spoiled it,
That sixtynine queer thieves who had AIDS
Were crucified, that the Croats so loved the world,
That the lady from Ecuador cut his cock off
Because she loved him,
That Ollie North has both cock and balls
And is seeking a seat
In the United States Senate
Which is filled
With cocks and balls,
O, West Virginia!
Now let us have a discussion About that kid from
the heartland of America
Who killed seventeen boys and ate them (not
    whole),
Grilled, fried, boiled and broiled.
He was a good boy, a little confused,
Said the nun, the priest, the teacher, his mother
    speaking for his father
Who had killed himself learning of his son's
    unfortunate deed.

Still and all
He must talk,
To the man who talks.
She is shy and listens.

Lock and Load!
Let's be heard!
Talent on loan from God!
I feel so crazeeeeee!
I am a liberal with sanity!
Ease up! Ease up! Ease up;
Take a deeeep breath, that's it.
The show is over, The monkey's dead. Sue ya!

The man dials.
The screener asks:
Are you there?
The man stammers.
The screener hangs up.
But the man is there.
His wife is there.
The kids are there
And they are giggling.
Talk is cheap.

Talk is money.
Talk, in its particles, fills the air.
All day talk.
All night talk.

Boil and bubble.
With out warning
The radio leaped
From the bedside table
And crashing, exploding, singing
The hit aria from Pagliacci, died.
The radio, what a mess,
Was more than its parts.
The radio, what a mess,
Was less than its parts.
That was the actual day the music died.
Talk, talk, talk, talk, talk, talk!
Then, wtihout warning
God on a very short wave
Descended and resurrected
The shattered white, plastic cube.
God extended his arm and said:

Let there be music!
And, although they could not be seen,
A thousand angels sang. And danced.
On abcnycorevdmcainscbs
The talkers picked the plastic from their teeth
Swallowed some cold coffee and continued . . . .

3. I Don't Want To Explain

I don't want to explain any more.
It does no good. Often, it does evil.
It is the sudden cold wind which freezes
The blue bird of happiness in flight.
I don't want to explain any more.
It does no good. Explanations kill.
Even though you found me snoring
In bed with big titted Shari,
I tell you we didn't do anything.
And my shorts on the floor,
What does that prove?
And what if once I have sinned?
Shall I explain myself to sainthood?

4. The Obits of the New York Times
A complaint to the editors

Somalia or the former Yugoslavia
Or the War neatly fixed on the Black Wall
Or the Gorbachevs of gloom (smile)
Or the Keystone spies and counter spies
Who kill with such all thumbs blitheness.
(Excusez-moi, cher Gaston was that your back
Which fell so fatally on my blade?)
Today, only today, all murders and rapes
Will be relegated to the rear
After the unemployment listings.
I forgive you for fucking up.
For the news comes so swiftly
Screaming to the screen.
And your intern crew of children
Struggles so to put each blip to bed.
I forgive you for fucking up
The living and dying world.
For it is not easy to be
The Pravda of the Western World.

But you, joyless Warden of those stiffs
Floating face down and downward
On the cold, viscous, inky Styx,
I do not forgive.
Oh, the lips and cheeks are tenderly rouged,

The believable smile is appropriately fixed!
And Oh, the corpse properly garbed
In pin-striped suit or flowery wedding gown,
Is put eternally to bed
In Section B or D, reserving C for Arts.
All of this dressing is superficial.
So, I do not forgive you, O, Warden!
I do not forgive you for Mort Shuman's shroud,
Plucked threadbare from the Paris AP wire,
While in your morgue his reams of songs were
    singing.
Oh, Warden, save the last dance for him!
Nor Tom McGrath's memorial, two twisted inches,
Wrapping away his fifty years of poems like fish.
Blues For Tommy, A Real Gone Guy!
Yet, you give all nine obituary yards
To the pickle maker who funded a wing
For the Hospital of The Flying Christ,
And a thousand miles to the last living corporal
Who sloshed along with amoebic dysentary
On the Long March where, at the end,
He received a medal from Mao, a Little Red Book
And a pension for life
Transferable to his heirs and his assigns.
But those millions of heros
On longer marches to uncertain destinations
Who died the moment they got there
And were noted only

By black bordered Hallmark cards
On which the Postal Services profited
(Or lost money) by their deaths.
No tragedy here, O, Warden of the Obituaries,
For no matter how slightly,
The end of them is noted,
No matter how stiffly,
A curtain of tears shimmers down
And bathes them all away,
I will forgive you for forgetting their deaths.
If you will tell me who might I forgive
For forgetting their lives.

5. On This Island
On this island which lies
Slightly southeast of Hiva Oa
The beautiful olive women
No longer bare their breasts.
The beautiful olive men
Have put on thin blue jeans
And the official T-shirts
Of the fallen New York Knicks.

A raft arrives without fail
At the island shore
Every Monday morning.

It is laden with riches,
The goods of the world.

The beautiful olive women
Find the pink brassieres.
The beautiful olive men
Find the water proof watches
Which the groupers, with alarm, have read.
The olive men and the olive women
Sit up late at night
By the edge of the sea
Talking. Trying to find
A use for these things.

Last night, sitting in the ring
Of palms, they spoke seriously:
What might they do with the shame?
Why was it not in a plastic wrap?
Or in an appropriate box?
Does it come in all sizes?
Does one size fit all?

6. By Two Thousand Thirty Six

By two thousand thirty six
The Holocaust had been forgotten.
Not the event itself
Only the meaning of the event itself.
Outside Auchwitz Disney opened a new World

The World out drew the Jews
Four hundred eighteen to one.
The ones who went into the other place
Were given pamphlets explaining what it meant.
It seemed so silly to give all this importance
To an oven or a gurney with broken wheels.
Yad Vashem didn't fare much better.
Critics complained
It was the fault of the artists
Mainly the sculptors (too abstract).
Next the painters (representationless).
You couldn't tell a charred corpse
From a chicken feather.
Other critics complained:
How many corpses can you recreate?
How many surviving sets of bones?
How many tons of genuine dust?
Historians were not helpful here.
For nine years the chemical industry debated
    if it should fabricate an odor of burning flesh
To be released at selected memorials and
    museums.
It was voted down, narrowly,
On the grounds that the odor
Might not seem much different
Than Los Angeles air (Circa 1980)
Secondly, there was no money in it.
So the problem was turned over to the poets

110

Who protested vigorously
That they were not responsible for the Holocaust
And, besides, it was more likely a job for
    composers.
The composers took a very solemn and
    respectful Ad
In the *The New York Times* which said:
    (in essence)
Beethoven had already done it.

Protesting, one violinist,
Who represented no one but himself
Attached a batch of plastique to his fiddle
And drawing his bow across
(A high *A* above a High *C* ,
A scream of sorts)
Blew himself up.
The third string music critic
Of *The Times*, a stringer, actually,
Gave the event two paragraphs
And got the fiddler's name wrong.

Also there was the poet
Who represented no one but himself.
Who created an ode
Which created an absolute sensation
Thereby, outdrawing Disney.
The poem was made completely

Of question marks, one each to a line
Cruelly barbed like fishhooks
Which he wrote and rewrote
In red chalk on the sidewalk.
Every time he made his hook
He bled, sometimes from his ears,
Sometimes from his eyes,
Twice from his rectum.

He did this for thirty six days
And thirty six nights
And then he died.
The Times said he was a fake
And called for a special prosecutor.

7. The Rage of the Lawyer

When the mad man came to him,
His long knife dripping blood,
The lawyer said: Not on my desk!
The mad man said: O, excuse me.
Sternly now, the lawyer barked:
Why did you cut her
From vagina through sternum,
Remove her head and arms?
Sterner still the mad man hissed:
I was pissed off.
The eyes of the advocate widened.
Pissed off? The barrister repeated.

So pissed off, said the mad man,
I can't tell you. Very big pissed off.
The attorney circled his desk,
Nine times, in long strides
When he stepped into the pool on his rug.
Oh shit! The counsellor shouted.
The mad man said, No, blood.
The lawyer, his jaws setting, asked:
Pissed off?
Yes, said the mad man, very big, huge,
    humongous!
The lawyer, stentorian flags flying,
Said: It is the rage of mankind!
Pissed off! Pissed off! Pissed off!
I will take your case!
Pro Bono? asked the mad man.
Yes, said the lawyer, *Pro Bono.*
Now give me your knife.
No, said the mad man.

The next day they stood before the judge.
The lawyer pleaded the mad man innocent
On the well soaked grounds of *Pissed Off*
Which had first appeared in the draft of the Magna
    Carta
Although it had been struck in the published
    version.

8. *A Theme*

A theme. A subject.
Something splendidly huge.
Big enough for a university
Associate Professor to notice.
Maybe the big bang.
Maybe you.
Maybe last night
When you were the universe.

9. *The Harvard Psychiatrist*

The head of psychiatry
At Harvard in Boston said
There was no doubt
About the existence
And the activities
Of Extra Terrestrials.
He had patients
Who had been very much involved.
Each had seen the milk white forms,
The oval heads, the pools of eyes.
The Harvard psychiatrist
Added a footnote:
It is true, he said
I have other patients who long
For Extra Terrestrials
But, have encountered none
And they are dying of it.

10. Lecture at W.C. Fields University, 2689 A.D. Professor Dukenfeld Speaking

Language like liquor has its limits, yasss.
Explain that to the grey stone
Under the third leg of the billiard table
Innocently keeping the balls level, yasss.
Explain to that grey stone
That billions got killed, billions, yasss.
A voice from the rear,
A billion what?
What Weisenheimer asked that question?
Listen, Skinny, a billion of anything is significant.
In this here particular case
I think it was people, yasss,
A billion people, yasss.
Can't be sure. It was long ago.
Little Girl there, pretty little thing,
Run down to the commisary
And fetch me another bottle of Milk Weed,
The 220 proof.
I'm down to my last dram, yasss.
Run off now, my little Chickadee!

Explain to the grey stone
Under the second leg of the pool table, yasss,
How the world is *peised* well
Made to run even upon even ground.

Shakespeare, yasss,
Thank you for the Milk Weed, Little Girl,
No, sweetheart, you didn't miss much.
I'm gawna give you an A for running.
See me after class, clean the blackboards. yasss.
Oh, yasss, about the billion. Maybe it was less.
Japan, Rooshia, U.S. and A. Bosnia, Somalia,
Etcetera, etcetera, etcetera, etcetera.
It all adds up. You sure this is 220, Little Girl?
The billion, yasss. Their names were written
　　down. Somewhere. Where the hell is my cue
　　stick?
Yasss, written down, small but neat,
On the back of a large postage stamp.
Maybe I mailed a letter. Yasss, maybe I did that.
Any one see my cue stick?
A billion, yasss, a billion.
That's an important fact, kiddo.
A poet, yasss, a poet!
His name was on the back of the stamp.
Maybe he was an accountant,
Yasss, that's it, yasss.
He wrote: But the shining ones,
The once laughing ones,
They are the myriads gone.
Gone into dust and ash
If not into useful oil.

Yasss, y'notice he got the oil into it?
Which sonuvabitch stole my cue chalk?

The Anthropology Department has some skulls
And some red vintage telephones
But they haven't gotten a connection between the
    two.
Yasss.

I'm going to bank the cue ball.
A combo of the four into the eight
Into the corner pocket, yaaas.
Yasss, Skinny? What has the cue chalk
Got to do with grey stones?
Whalll, I haven't figgered that part out.
But I'll tell you this, Skinny:
As long as the table is level
Don't explain anything to a grey stone.
You might break its heart. Yasss.

11. Crimes of the State

It is the ruler's business to destroy,
It is the parliament's business to devour.
It is the bureaucrat's business to giggle
In the purring corridors of the computer rooms.
They should be respected.
They do their jobs.
They are not clock watchers.
They are to be forgiven
An occasional puff, pop or belt
Or for fucking in the broom closet.
It is only tenderness they lack.
After all they are not crocodiles
Nor are they great white sharks.
Give us this day our daily bread,
They sometimes say that.

12. Here's to the Hookers and Porno Queens Of East Sodom, New Jersey

I wonder if they had learned
All the dirty secrets
When they were still children?
Or later, when nubile and menstrual.
How did they know
That there were producers, photographers,
        publishers and pornographers
Ready to prurify the prurient world?

More important
How did they know there was *money* in it?
Knowledge is sin.*
Last year eleven hookers,
Seven XXXX movie stars,
All residents of East Sodom,
Male and female, were murdered.
But not one of them
Had turned to salt.**
(Janet Reno is investigating.)
How do hookers know all this?
How did the dead ones know
What the priests and the presidents know?
Why is the underside of the universe
Common knowledge to all except the innocent?

* See Genesis   ** See Crimes of the State

13. There Are No Crimes Left
There are no crimes left,
No blood to let,
No laws to enact.
The end of the world is on hand.
But the lawyers and the doctors
And the happy politicians
All set their alarm clocks
Rise up at the bell

Catch their trains, go to work.
Like the lillies of the fields
They bend in the winds,
They voice activate
The prioritized dials,
Hello, I must be going.
Clients die, patients expire,
The orations are loud and proud.
The doctors and the lawyers
And the political chiefs
Look warily from their windows
At the gang of men paving the road.
The open happiness of labor,
The laughter of asphalt!
The singing, the dancing, the beer!
No easy task to fill out
The long deposit slip
And take it to the bank
Around the corner.

14. April Something, 1994

It's fifty years since Hitler died.

I think the Jews have gotten the joke.

You've got to like guys with a sense of humor.

The above does not qualify as a haiku.

It's also one syllable more than a triple chai.

It's a new dive off the high board of perfect love.

The memory of pain does not endure.

15. Gain Be My Lord For I Will Worship Thee

The CEOs of the narcotics industry

Stand before the Congressional Committee.

The Chairman, weeping, asks:

Why have you done it?

The tallest of the CEOs asks:

Done what?

Chairman: You know, alcohol, heroin, crack,
nicotine, angel dust, designer drugs.

The Shortest: You left out sunshine. The people
want it: the stuff, y'know.

Chairman: The people are dying, sir!

The Fattest: Let them die. It's good for them.

Chairman: How dare you!

Fattest: I'm telling you the truth. Without death

We'd have nothing left but taxes.

Tallest: And the alleged poor.

Shortest: Good point! *Alleged!*

Where do the so-called poor get the crack
money?

Chairman: You snake! They sell their bodies and
their souls!

Tallest: Good point, sir!

There's a market for those things, too.

Chairman: For bodies and souls?

Tallest: Yes, sir! Bodies if they're young. Souls, all
the time.

Fattest: We must all stand together, Mr. Chairman.

We stand or fall on the bottom line.

Shortest: This is the greatest system in the world,
sir!

Tallest: Can you deny that?

Chairman: I don't deny that.

Tallest, Shortest, Fattest: So what the fuck are we
doing here?

Chairman: There was a reason. What was the
reason?

16. Let Me Now Praise Theatre

The Shuberts should have known
It was a short way from Les Miz
To Minnie Mouse.
The Nederlanders knew all the time
That Disney had turned
A thousand dalmatians loose
Sniffing along old Broadway
Finding the piss spoor of the money trail.
Coveting T.S. Eliot's Cats
The Disney Dawgs and Beasts
Chased the Jujamcyns to the banks
Where they closed their accounts
And sold their temples for twofers.
Would you believe Mickey Mouse
At a hundred ten dollars a ticket?
Was that the day the music died?
Was that the day the National Endowment Fund
    For the Arts
Denied a grant to a team of exterminators
For the gilding of three thousand
Brown urban beetles.

17. The Poetry of Silence

When the printers inked the type
And rolled his words beneath
The heavy blessing of the press,
He became, in the world of poems,
Actual.
Reading and rereading he was repelled.
The black handed printer
Had spoiled the lines,
Had lifted the lightness,
Had diminished the song.
So, in the Cafe of the Celestial Worm
He mounted the butcher table
And sang his flesh
To the tune of his soul.
Some one bought him an espresso.
Some one said, Good Work!
So, in the Cafe of the Celestial Worm
He took the far corner chair,
Took a vow of silence
And set the song spinning
Inside his onanistic head
Where the frozen poem was perfect.
He was actual, in tune,
Alone.

18. A Note to H. Dumpty
Perhaps in your day
You tyranized words
But you fell and there you were,
Thoroughly untogether.
But in our day
Words tyranize us
And we fall where we stand
Hardboiled and crazed
And as thoroughly together
As a permafrost.

19. Let Us Now Praise Marshal Petain, Let Bygones Be Bygones*
He was a hero, of course,
In the manner only the French declare them.
He was well decorated, of course,
With a chestful of iron designs.
He had collaborated with the enemy, of course,
With class and dignity, however.
He was found guilty of treason, you remember,
But forgiven because he was very old.

*A memory of 1945

20. On Broadway White Beggars

On Broadway white beggars
Do better than black.
But I never discriminate.
Beggary is color blind, I say.

I give nothing but a smile
To the black cup shaker.
I give nothing but a smile
To the extended white palm.

I detest the donor who gives
A dime to the one
While flipping a quarter,
Fraternally, to the other.

21. Paradise Was A Manageable Place

Paradise was a manageable place for Milton
He could explore it while blind.
He could lose it and find it all in a day.
But, it seems to me, in these times
Paradise lurks behind a cumulocirrostratus
Where the angels sit beneath umbrellas and pout.
Manageable, still, but unbearably cute.

22.

Rwanda.
A name woven of silk
Soft as your kiss,
Warm as your blood.

23. *Lines for Calvin Klein*

Some men are breast men
Some arouse at derrieres
Some crack up at crotches
Dressed in little beards.
But Klein, no Calvinist,
Keeps each on his denim list.
Some sell and others buy,
The jailed poet cried.
But I am not a simp
If I buy I am a john
If I sell I am a pimp.

24. D-Day + Fifty Years
A Memory of Inland England

In the cottage behind the castle
I spent my three day pass in your bed.
How kind you were to me and America!
We never heard the guns,
Never dreamed of the blood on the beaches.

25. A Long Story Very Much Shortened

Born in Vienna at the wrong time
She ran to Buenos Aries
Two jumps ahead of the assassins.
There she married and made love
Until her husband's brain became
The jellied cave of a boulder
Which grew and grew
And ate him up from the inside.
So, daughter in tow, she fled again
To the America of sure tomorrows.
She found a Russian lover in New York.
Her daughter, a crack and cocaine head,
OD'd in Riverside Park on the rock
Where Edgar Allan Poe sometimes sat.
Now walking her dying dog along
The shady side of Broadway
She thought she was a fortunate woman.
She had reached the age of eighty-one

And felt, she was sure, better than the dog.
She had two friends still alive.
One was ninety three, the other ninety six.
Both had their wits about them.
This was quite encouraging:
She could see her future
And it did not seem at all bad

26. A Book Is Written About T.S. Eliot's Early Thoughts

The French Resistance fellows threw a party
For you and me and I remember it vaguely:
Pour Les Deux Poetes Americaines.
Picasso was there and Aragon.
I spent my time with them: you scared me.
You called me an *effete* New Yorker
And I didn't know, then, what *effete* meant.
You told Masson he was a British *subject.*
Masson said, "For you the niggers always
    begin on the other side of Calais."
Devastating.
Eluard, pale and weary, avoided you, too
And stood with Nouche in a private corner.
Air alarm sirens sounded.
A mistake, the enemy had abdicated.

I wondered why you had crossed the
     Channel at all.
Did you need this honor to wash away your sins?
Fifty years later a scholar examines your thoughts,
Those thoughts you had in 1925 and 1933,
Not your thoughts that night in Paris.
I think everyone who attended the party
Is dead now, myself excepted, of course.
And you, Thomas, may not have crossed
To Heaven or to Hell but you have become
An ivy covered cottage light industry,
The leaves thick, brown and odorless.

27. Roots, Branches, Questions

Word came to Avenue D
That his father had died
In the town of Koscord
In 1939 Hungary.

He rent his garment
And ran down the Street,
Mourning the father
He had lost long ago.

Before the dreaded Nazis
The comfortable neighbors came
Rounding everybody up
Bolting them inside their synogogue
To wait for the black train.

They are all gone now.
I am here on 92nd Street
A half a town away,
A half a century away
From Ninth Street and Avenue D.
Cut off and burned to char
My roots are there
Where I will never go.

I wonder what Matthew thinks?
Am I to him both root and branch?
Was Alexander who ran his tears dry
My root, my branch, my violin?

28. On Perusing a Magazine of Poetry
It seems constantly the same:
Passings and pastorals.
Love near the lake where the loon laughs.
The inventors of the sui generic sorrow
Find in the mornings or evenings
Their souls in flight. No harm done.

Poetry can be pushed down any highway.
It is to drive a car that one needs a license.

29. *Lines for Dennis Potter*
One ear cocked to an era you hardly knew
You played a Hit Parade of scratchy tunes.
Kafka imagined the man in the cockroach
And you inside your dripping red exoskeleton
Whistled the metaphor of man as lobster
Scuttling along the bottom,
Throwing up mysterious, abrasive clouds.

30. *Rosh Hashona, 1994 C.E.*
In New York on the fashionable West Side
Where it was utterly safe
For Jews to worship
The parades to the vanishing synogogues
Thinned out.

In Crown Heights, the zone of the Chassidim,
Where life was perilous
For Jews to worship
The parades to the enduring synogogues
Thickened.

31. *A Visit With Pablo Picasso, 1945*

Suddenly, he left his easel
And walked slowly to the wall
Where the dry canvas leaned.
With the hot vermillion on the brush
He rouged her misplaced lips again.
I thought, I said, that one was done.
Alas, he said, No painting is finished
Until it is priced and taken away
To be abandoned in a crowd.

32. *Some Questions for Stephen Hawking*

What if God was bad at math?
Could he have big banged and expanded?
What if you were bad at math?
Could you see the universe smooth or rough?
And if there is a birthing singularity
Isn't the breath of God enough?
And if there is, indeed, imaginary time
Which is only the real time
Which we invented because there was nothing
    there
Are we locked in the bubble (imaginary)
Which Tweedle Dee dreamed
Wondering what would happen
If the Dreamer awoke?

33. The Voices He Hears

I do not doubt that they are loud, Peter.
Although scattering through the static
Of your mind; the brain twittering.
My objection, if any, is the uselessness.
Voices without direction, trailing off
Into the long wilderness of abandonment.
Joan of Arc, at least, did it for God and Country.
You do it for no one
Yet, like her, you burn at the stake.
She, brightly, with a rapid ascent to heaven.
You, with your smoke and mirrors
And the rusty ticking and scraping
Of a stained clock,
The hands stuck together.

34. In Memoriam

Today I wrote my own obit.
Some of it true, most of it shit.

35. An Encounter

I have read you in remainders, she said.
In which particular years? I asked.

36. Singing A Song
The day is soft with close clouds
And mists which cling to windows.
It is a day when New York thinks
It is Paris, my Paris, my 1945 Paris
After the Germans had packed their tanks
And had gotten out of town.
The mist is on my face
Like wet laughter. I am walking!
I am singing a long forgotten Gold Oldie
Which never made the Hit Parade.

It was six o'clock in the morning
When Sweeney came around
With a piece of bread and butter
Which weighed a half a pound!

Here we go marching
The boys of Carey Camp
Are on their way!
Give a cheer for the camp,
Give a cheer for the camp,
Give a cheer, give a cheer,
Give a cheer for the camp!

It was six o'clock in the morning
I looked upon the wall
The bedbugs and the roaches
Were having a game of ball.
The score was six to nothing
The roaches were ahead
A bed bug hit a homer
And knocked me out of bed!
Here we go marching, etc.

A young woman smiling
Falls in with my stride.
She asks, Is that a song from your times?
I answer, *These are my times!*
I whistle my way down to 72nd Street.
The mist lifts. There is the sun.

An Old Man's Poem
Or the Anteroom
1996

1. *Something I've Forgotten*

Something I've forgotten. . . . .
But there's the thing: what?
Nothing's burning on the stove.

I smell things that burn, thank God.
I open the heavy white door.
Cold hand into cold space.
Plastic pouches, crisp and clean
Sour dough has not turned green.
Nothing spoiling in the fridge, thank God!
Something I've forgotten. . . what?

The window against the winter rain
Is closed. Is it? I'll look again.
Closed.
Outside, umbrellas only go uptown.
The regular rainy Broadway miracle.
I'm distracting myself.
Uptown, I mustn't dwell on uptown.
Something I've forgotten; it's alright.
Yes, yes, it's alright!
My voice! I can't hear my voice.
Where has my voice gone, is it lost?
Or did I forget my voice?

Mother, can you hear me?
That sounded alright.
Crisp as the lettuce in the plastic pouch.

I'd like to select what to forget:
Mad Peter drugged in the grey towers
In his unmatched socks, sidewinding
Across the deck painted floors
Of the insane asylum floating on the river
Where he howls silently, drools like an ocean,
Dripping from the nesting rocks.
I'd like to select what to forget:
Paul in the private desert of desire
Where the homsine grinds the rainbow down
Into the magic sand of gels and caps and rocks,
His skull drooling.
I'd like to kick his ass,
Dying that way in his wrecked and wretched room.
Instead I cry. Unfair, unfair!
But perhaps I'm lucky: four sons
And only two devoured by monsters!
In the south room the sun paints my eyes white.
White, a mysterious white.
White, warm and white.
My unrefrigerated hand opens the far door.
It creaks and swoons back on its hinges.

I have never been in this room before.
My heart pounds. I think:
Some one has just built this room.
It is a pent room, an anteroom.
It is a very white room.
Or did I forget this room?
Something I've forgotten, but what?

There is the nothing in the anteroom.
There is nothing on the white walls,
Not even a calendar.
There are two chairs and a couch.
They have no color; they are just themselves.
I sit in one chair. The other is empty.
The couch is empty. There is a ticking
But there is no clock. It is time breathing;
Inspiring, expiring. Nothing to read.
Two doors, faintly present in the walls.
They are unmarked but I know them.
One goes to my future
Which is, of course, my death.
The other goes to my past
Which is, of course, my life.
I can not rise up from my chair
To go toward my life.
I do not want to go toward
My certain future.
So I do not move.

Truth is old rheumatiz has got me.
I *can't* move.
But the room is shrinking,
Imperceptably shrinking.
I can not see that. I percieve it.
The weightless hair on my arms tinkles
Like bells I feel but do not hear.
There is so much to do, but what?
What did I forget? What?

Maybe the river is what I forgot.
No. I have not forgotten it.
I hear it wrapping itself
Around the deep green legs
Of the Ninth Street Pier.
I smell it on the wind
In the red brick canyons of childhood.
Then, of a sudden, it is there
With its lap and suck.
And I am there,
Naked on the splintered dock,
In a sun so pure
That the blues and whites
Of heaven are blinded by it.
Oh God, I want to weep,
Weep, to think that I was naked there!
Pure. Whole. My curling hair burning.
Oh, Milton, were you there, too?

You are so vague, Miltie.
Half an orphan, you were lost on Fourth Street,
Already scared and scarred and smiling.

Forgot what? Not the dock, not the river.
Not you, Miltie. Not Estelle.
Does she remember the pier, the river, the night
I put my hand inside her shirt,
Turned her nipples
In my intelligent hand
Which signalled the opening of the gate.
That gate! I have not forgotten that,
Nor the key inserted.
How the world moaned!
And where is Junie?
And where is Sally? Hindi? Mindi and Miriam,
Mossy gates ajar?

On the dock, off the dock, you, me,
Broad wooden planks, grey potpourri.
The bouquet of the river salt,
The sun salt, the air salt,
All pouring upward into the sky
Which needs the universe merely to exist.

But I've forgotten something. What?

2. The Rain Stopped;
I Descend Into The Street
I stumble over the body of a derelict
Buried alive in his corrugated casket.
Beneath my old mustache I ask,
Whose son are you?
A rivulet of piss emerges
From the cardboard teepee.
It skirts my shoe.
Respect for age, eh?
He's not Mapplethorp's Christ
But obscene all the same
And is equally not to be funded next year.
Pure, unfunded, stinking, invisible,
The symbol of nothing. Nothing. Nothing at all.
Shit on the sidewalk to be flushed away
When the New York rain starts again.
Flushed away! The shit, the box of death,
The trembling homunculus,
The once bitten green bagel
Dropped by St. Patrick
Busy leading snakes away
Along Broadway going south.
I forget all this before 72nd Street.
That's not it, of course.
Something else, something else. What?

3. At The Famous Dairy Restaurant
I Have These Thoughts

The anchor made of two stones
Deliberately dropped from the pier
Through Schriller's floating corpse,
As soft as soaked bread.
The anchor of accidental stone
Falling through Schriller's improvised existence
Down into the accepting sea.
I have never forgotten that.
I have never wanted to remember it.
Never. It was *real* without meaning.
It is the overture to all urban nightmares,
The reprise of all songs
Basso profundo politicians sing.
O, Say Can You See, Allons Enfants De Patrie,
Arise Ye Prisoners of Starvation, Has Any One
Seen My Bow Wow, Bow Wow etc.

I will pay my bills today, perhaps.
Ah, Con Ed never forgets,
Hardly ever forgives. *Ora Pro Nobis!*
Christ On His Wooden Rocket. . . . .
But no one ever held a match to that holy tail
To send the bleeding boy to Heaven.
Tom, Tom, forever the device of memory!
Forever his ashen self,
Hardly filling half an urn,

Turned, maybe, in a cheap Japanese mill.
And myself, leaving tomorrow's urn unfilled:
Am I the device of forgetfulness?

4. Who Built My White Anteroom?

Who built my white anteroom?
There are magazines in white wicker cradles.
The covers and the pages also white,
All the words engraved in white,
The literate blind reading as we watch
Their white mice hands scattering
Across the flat calligraphy,
A white maze where the leaves shatter
As the sightless duo
With their wet blind thumbs turn the pages,
To peruse these obscure histories,
Engraved but deeply unwritten there.

Ah, anteroom!
Not a nail on which to hang a single life!
Everything must be forgotten here,
Even my white self.
there in the middle of the white air
The white sign says:
To Remember Is To Live.
Remember what? What have I forgotten?

5. *I Try To Remember Pearl Harbor, Omaha Beach, And Other Resorts*

The post card came in the morning mail.
All along Ninth Street there was silence.
Who spoke? Who wept?
Who shook the wrinkles
Out of the unboxed flag?
I filled to the very top,
With clean socks and underwear,
The paper bag (my mother's wish).
The paper bag once filled
With Moshe's famous *tzitzel* bread
And the deep odor of the *chernishkas*
Which must outlast a hundred years of death.
Goodbye Mama, goodbye Papa,
Goodbye my sisters and my brothers, too:
I'm going for a soldier!

Why am I running headlong away
From Avenue D?
Why am I climbing ramparts?
Who put them there?
Why are the catapults hurling
The metal truth into the fleshy night?
What am I running toward?

How white it is in this room!

6. On A Train Going North It Occurs To Me That My 76th Birthday Comes The Next Day

Seventy-seven is a destination
Reached, finally, across wide landscapes
Across boundless plains,
Beneath a fog which insinuates itself
Between earth and heaven.

The wheat heads raise stiffly up
To hear the far whistle.
In its roots it feels
The train's deep song rolling under boulders
Pocked by the light of the masked sun.
The steel wheels suck the space
Beneath the heavy weight of burden.
The mist parts, coils, genuflects.
Not related to the tracks,
Whooo . . . Whooo . . . Whooo!
Around the bend of time the train comes.
Strong asthmatic scream . . . . .

The whispering train slits through
The diamond beaded air.
The passengers in their assigned seats
Beneath the unrevealing yellow lights,
Fold back the leaves of immediate histories
Bud do not read.

Two conductors are taking tickets.
One smiles. The other frowns.
But all tickets are punched
Or, worse, taken away and replaced
By a laundry list of frightened towns.
A passenger asks: Is this the train to Scarsdale?

The gray light and the thin armed trees scratch
Patterns across the fog bearing glass.
Noisily, light and branches break and fall.
The passengers lean forward, tense with listening:
Nothing. The sighing of mortality, perhaps.
Anxiously they peruse the minutely printed schedule.
It is clear: This train will be exactly on time.
They are sure of the final destination
But pray fervently never to arrive
So they sing something Catholic.

Time. Train. Fog. Continuous hissssssss.
An Angel reads the fading schedule
Over my shoulder. You seem so full of life, she says,
Why do you continuously contemplate being dead?
I don't, I say, I think about Nothingness.
Ha, Ha! Contradicteth the winged being.
I smile, I say, The cold universe,
The eternity of ice, the Nothingness.
Ha, Ha! she saith.

I saith in reply I do not understand it
But it is beautiful. It is deep black.
No, no, the sparkling Angel says: It is deep white!
White! That's right, of course (me talking)
It is the deep white which cups the eyes.
Nothingness.
Oh, no, she says, It is the Life which fills you.
The Life you sing. The laughter Life. The sadness
    Life.
The Life of many colors. Animals and seas.
Woodlands. Wastelands. Wheatlands.
Stars. Moons. Comets. Men. Women. Children.
You.
Me?
Yes, you too, Old Person.

Whiteness is deathness.
Wrong! Whiteness is Lifeness.
Forget the fucking color!
Where's my father gone
And where's my mother gone?
Tom knew. They've gone into the white wood
Before me
Or up the Grandfather stairs into the white attic
Which gives up the smell of time
As slowly as fragrant grass
Inside an alabaster jar mislaid by an Egyptian girl.

150

I worry about you, Old Person! Too much death in
    you.
Don't worry silly girl, I'm alive still.
I praise my hands. I praise my eyes. I praise my legs
And my testicles.
And if I leave them jewels to you, kiddo,
Where would you keep them?

Time. Train. Fog. Continuous hisssss.
What have I forgotten aside from these dreams?

7. I Am Confronted By My Grandfather's Ghost

Why have you come into this room?
To see you.
But you do not know me?
I know you. You are Sandor's son.
How do you know that?
The dead know many things.
Sandor is dead. Speak to Sandor.
He excommunicated me.
Because you were a mean Hungarian!
Did he say that? That I was mean?

(He howls and he moans. He puts down his head.
White tears flow down his white vest.)

I loved him. Didn't he know that?
No.
Was it because of that strumpet, Juliana?
Juliana was my mother.

(For a long time my grandfather weeps.
The white tears fall like beads of ice.
He stares at me through his empty white eyes.)

She was an ignorant peasant, this Juliana.
Sandor could have married a Princess!
He was in love.
He gave me up for her? For this Juliana?
Yes. For my mother.
Not one word! Excommunicated!
You're a mean man! Why have you come to me?
He will not talk to me. My son will not speak to me!

(How can a howl be so loud in a white room?
He tramples his tears, white grapes of remorse,
Grapes frozen on the vine of early winter.)

What was his fate in the New World?
He became a taxi driver. He lost his kidneys.
He lost his teeth. He brought home some coins.
Juliana turned the coins into white curtains.
Into loaves and fishes and *polacinta*

On certain nights your son sat on a cushion
And Juliana, serving him, said he was a prince.
Did he know that I died?
Yes. He rent his garments
He ran through the streets,
Howling!

Ah, ah, ah . . .

He fades away,
Lajos of Koscord fades away.

Sandor was a sweet man
Sandor was a kind man
Sandor was a tender man
Sandor had love in him

I am too much like Lajos.

5. The Phone Doesn't Ring Much, Any More
In the white room on the white wall
There is the imperceptible white phone,
Useless unless it rings.
In the young days, the fine man days,
It rang so often it was rigged
With two call-waitings. The world stood on line!
— Hello there! Is this you?
— Me, all right. I love you, baby,
But speak fast. My agent's on the horn!

— Hello there! Is it you, Erico?
— You got me, baby, but talk fast,
The President is waiting.
— Hahaha! Don't kid me, you old kidder!
— I ain't kidding, kid, it's the Prez!
— You've got it made, you old sonuvabitch!
You're sitting on top of the world!
— Hahaha! Call me next week!
Now the wire hums. I hurt his feelings.
Whose feelings? I can't remember.
Did I hurt your feelings?
I really did not intend it.
Call any time, any time; any time, please.
Are you all in my white room?
Are you here waiting for my call?
No, the room is empty if you don't count
Near sighted old men.
I understand why the white room is empty.
It is preparing me for graduation;
White mortar boards, great music!

After two wholly silent days
The white phone rings.
I get to it. There is nobody there.
Why did I take so long?

Today I called The Operator and complained:
The white telephone in the white room
Does not ring.
It will, says The Operator, Be patient.

This is my voice, you know.
It has a crack in it, the operator says.
It is only a very small crack, I say.
But the operator knows it will widen.

Wasn't I kind enough?
Didn't I respond to your need?
Call please! Please call.
Please call while there is time.
Do you think that they have changed my number?
That's it! Tomorrow I shall send out cards!

Dust gathers on the coiled wire.
It is white dust.
The kind you find in Egyptian tombs.

6. Self Pity

No one will miss me when I am gone.
No one loves me for myself alone.
There are three billion people on the globe.
Who gave the masked killer the key to my home?
Why am I left alone and crying?
I want to be brave,

Noble and neatly shaved
When I say to the doctor:
No heroic measures, please!

But I've forgotten something.
Perhaps, the prompter will shout it out?
But he has gone to lunch.
His open script is face down
Nailed to the stage with duck tape.
Is it in the script?
Is this my play they are playing?
Am I in my play? And my role?
Myself? A bit part.
A bit part in the play of my life?
Is that what I forgot? Do I play myself?
Am I only a bit part?
No.
I will never remember what I forgot.
So, I will make it up.
I forgot to say, shall I go shopping today
I forgot to say, Do you want some soup?
I forgot to say, You are better than I.
I forgot to say, I wasn't completely bad.
I forgot to say, I was in the 221st
Signal Base Depot Company,
ETO, 1944, D–Day plus 29.
(The 222nd was dead in the water
On that hallowed Invasion Day.)

I forgot to say, The red wind blown banners
Were at my back and how I sang
The songs which shook the world!
I forgot to say, I love you.
Will that do, my dear?

It is so white in here.

The Second Wind
The Immortal Wind

The Second Wind, The Immortal Wind

1.

The second wind, the immortal wind
Spins across the mind and sighs:
This is it my old and beamish boy.
You have yet some days and nights
To dream and sort your times.
The second wind, the immortal wind
Sings in its hollow monotone:
Get your ass into joy's high gear
Let that choir of assembled days
Sing loud old cuckoo, sing loud!
The second wind, the immortal wind
Floats old banners on the air
Excelsior! Hoorah! Hoorah!
Once upon a memory
I was there and I am here.
Let me sing now of relative truth
For absolutes are too uncouth.

2.

Charles and Betty said,
"You deal too much with death."
And I thought, The Poor
Will always be with us
There always will be Taxes
And there always will be Death
Destiny, I thought, the Fate of Man.

Postulates all, I thought, graven
On my hard drive by God
Or by a near sighted girl
In some airless orient
Or is it a boy with tiny hands in Pakistan
Who ties the tightest knots
To make the sun bright carpet
On which I fly, immortal and amazed
Among the stars which burn
On dark oceans of weightless mass.
Do the dark, cold oceans stand for Death?
Do the burning islands stand for Life?
Listen, all I know is this: I am travelling.
Somebody bought me my ticket.
Oceans, islands, lights.
The girl who engraves me has a name.
The boy with tiny hands has a name.
Anonymity — that is death.

3.

Before the dawn by my own clock
I rise into the grey, undifferentiated
    light.
Good morning, God! How are you?
The white sui generic plastic bottle,
A syringe unto itself, releases with a sigh
One clear drop into my last failing eye.
Oh, it is a magical morning!

I listen for the scattering feet of the mice
Across the ancient (Nineteen oh seven)
Hard wood floors.
They racket as if they are wearing
   Timberland boots!
But I am awake and you are asleep
Making your own dry racket.
Later you will tell me your dream.
Amazing, always amazing! If I were you
I'd write them down and sell them to me.
Why don't I dream?

What if cockroaches were wearing the boots?
The sound of eight feet stomping.

In the kitchen warm and bright
I set the pot upon its light
Until the oat meal comes
Hot and steaming to the bowl.
(The above is poetry —more or less.
Old men can make such dawn decisions
Without the contradictions of pissy critics.
A poem is a poem because I declare it so.)
I sing softly and whistle the porridge cool.

Hark!
Now I hear the sound of the scattering boots
Across the white tile floor of the outer hall
Beyond my bolted door. A thump, a sigh!
Who dies there upon my barricade?

Only the noisy kid tossing
The fat *New York Times*
With its asthmatic splash.
The sonuvabitch is an hour early today.
I won't look at that rag until after eight o'clock.
Everything in the universe has its time and place
Even The Pravda of the gun shy West.

You are asleep.
I am awake.
This is my time.
This is my place.

Good Morning, God!
How are you?

4.

My father, Alexander, used to say
Be careful son, don't fall between two chairs.
Some people also said, You can't dance
At two weddings! Others, You can't serve
Two masters! Feel-good folk wisdom.
It was the awful fear of falling between the cracks.
Quick flashes of Heronymous, assorted horrors,
Assorted hells pierced by lute players
And tiny bare assed figures defecating
In Public Squares. Alas! Alack!
Falling, falling between the cracks!
There are universes down there
And undeveloped photographs of you
And there are thousands of shipwrecks
There is *The Titanic,* a gold mine of the dead,
And there is *The Slocum,* of no value at all.

5.

If I left you all my money
You could buy a Chinese meal
Or go to a movie, maybe.
Or you could skip the movie, maybe
Because although they change the titles
They never change the plot lines —
The hero survives, the villain dies
Boy meets girl, boy loses girl,
Boy finds girl, boy and girl go to bed

(Circa post 1960.)
The film editor knows this and sobbing
Weeps black and white tears.

William S. Hart and Rudolph Valentino
Eternally guard the Gates Of Hell.
It is not clear:
Are they keeping you from going in
Or keeping the hounds from coming out?
The film is very scratchy and in soft focus.
The editor in the dark is up to his ass
In negative philosophy. He fumbles around
For cold noodles and cardboard shrimp.

If I left you my wisdom
And my good advice
You might get a few good laughs
Without necessarily staying out of trouble.

If you choose among
These legacies I leave —
Take the Chinese,
Go to the movies.

6.

In my ear you are singing, always singing,
Tones as light as angels dancing.
The quality of singing is not strained . . .
You were singing because it was the only thing
You did profoundly well although you doubted
The worth of your hire and dwelt on that mystery.
Why did they hire you in the Borscht Circuit
To be crushed among the klezmers and comics?
And did the Russian owner say in French:
Qui a besoin des chansons francaises?
Or Brahms for that matter? You're fired!

But all was not lost because they hired you
To sing on the side show bally stand
Surrounded by bad toothed, big boobed strippers.
And they fired you because – remember? –
Take it off! Take it off! Take her off!
And oh my God, under the borrowed black cape,
You were wearing your Hallelujah Chorus gown,
The only performance gown you owned
And you had hardly any boobs at all!

But they didn't fire you
At Kornman's Back Room
They just ignored you, guitar and all,
Except two portly old sales men
Who came on with their worn merchandise.

Yet old Kornman wept as you sang
Thinking he had saved Detroit's soul.
All you could do was sing.
The tone was in you,
Fulfilled you, thrilled you,
Made you something more than nothing
And aside from your mailbox
Bulging with unpaid bills
Singing was the thing
And enough.

But existence is magic
The songs inserted themselves
And you were all cracked silver bells
And you were oracular,
Mea Culpa, Baby
The roar of the grease paint
The smell of the crowd . . .
Why did you flee fame like a fawn?
Why were the bravas discordant in your ears?
How did such beauty court such fear?
Would greatness turn your throat to dust?
Maybe to sing you had to wear
The cape of doubt on the bally stand of the world.

You marched from the wings to the microphone,
Stage center of the great hall.
At your feet the sign was laid

Chante Juste! it said.
You saw it. You smiled. You sang.

This is a love poem.

7. *The Old Performers Do A Benefit*

Betty Boston, the singer from Philadelphia,
Croaked out a medley of hits from the Thirties.
Tears flowed. Good applause.

Donald Detroit, the black tap dancer from Dallas
Put a live mike at his feet
And buck-and-winged past his arthritis.
Whistles and stomps. Very good applause.

Luis de Los Angeles from East Louisiana
Did his amazing slight of hand
Using very large playing cards
From which the spots fell on command
Into the orchestra pit.
Gasps. Shouts. Good applause.

Susan T. Savannah from South Dakota,
The famous Lady One Man Band
Cake Walked on stage
Clapping her cymbals
And Talking *Tea For Two*
Into her gold plated kazoo.

Between her two numbers
Susan T. explained that Chico
Her monkey had died that winter.
Then she did one helluva Swanee River
Played In Ragtime.
Piercing whistles. Very, very good applause.

It was my job to close the show.
The audience knew I was legally blind,
Deaf as a post and had two recent
Hip replacements.
But I got to my feet, looked out at the crowd,
And aimed myself at the microphone,
Where I *thought* the microphone was.
The lights bounced off my choppers.
The band played *Pomp And Circumstance*.
I went forward a steady step at a time
I got a tremendous standing ovation –
For Walking.

8. The Second Wind, The Immortal Wind, Encore

The second wind, the immortal wind
Calls all my darlings back to sing
The old unforgotten songs,
The golden oldies, the hit parade;
More ravishing than any tunes
That Walt or Will had ever played.

Oh, the list of those I've loved is long —
So long, my friends, so long!
I saw old Papa in the glass of shops
As I walked along the street.
I smiled at him, he smiled at me
Reflections always meet.

The second wind, the immortal wind
Whistles its catchy tune
And June and moon and soon
And every silly rhyme is fine
And in my mind we're dancing.
The second wind, the immortal wind
Floats me on its breath
Takes me on my daily walk
Far away from death!
Hut two three four
Hut two three four
This is the way we go to war.

This is the way the old men march
One eye to the pavement
One ear to the heart
The ancient body creaks down town
I'm alive in here! Are you alive out there?

The second wind, the immortal wind . . .